The
LAKE DISTRICT

Edward Alan Bowness

'The loveliest spot that man hath ever found'
William Wordsworth

Introduction

The Lake District became a National Park in 1951, and with an area of almost 900 square miles (2330 sq km) it is the largest in England and Wales. Originally composed of three counties, Cumberland, Westmorland and the Furness district of Lancashire, all that is best in Lakeland is now in the county of Cumbria. More picturesque and diverse scenery can be found here than in any comparable area of Britain.

Within 30 miles (48 km) one may range from the harsh crags of England's highest mountain, Scafell Pike, to the fertile lowland valleys around Winster, from the depths of great lakes like Wastwater to shallow blue tarnlets scattered like confetti on the top of Haystacks, from sparkling ghylls on the sides of Harrison Stickle to the roaring brown torrent of Duddon in flood.

For the lover of outdoor life, the Lake District has almost everything. The camper, the artist, the pony trekker, the yachtsman, the fisherman, the naturalist – Lakeland caters for them all. Some come for the quiet delights of trout fishing at the head of Windermere late on a June evening, as the sun sets between the twin peaks of the Langdales and the water becomes a black mirror. Others revel in the kaleidoscope of colour and noise which is a Lakeland sports meeting at Grasmere or Ambleside. In Langdale, expert cragsmen test their skill and courage against the rock faces of Gimmer or Pavey Ark, or cut January steps into frozen snow cornices on Bowfell.

Go in June through Manesty woods on Derwentwater's shore, and you would swear that nowhere could show so many shades of green. Visit again in October, and see the fox-red bracken above Watendlath, flaming in autumn sunshine. There are few finer days than those spent wandering the fells, to descend at dusk to a welcoming farmhouse, and enjoy Cumbrian food and hospitality.

Make your own memories, on foot if you can, when the June days are long, the clouds are high and the hills are free. Perhaps then you may say of Lakeland, as William Wordsworth wrote of Grasmere, that it is 'the loveliest spot that man hath ever found'.

BELOW: *Ramblers on Loughrigg Fell, overlooking Grasmere towards Helm Crag and the Easedale Valley.*

OPPOSITE: *Canoeists on the fast-flowing River Rothay at Rydal.*

OPPOSITE, LEFT INSET: *Pony riders in the Mickleden Valley near Dungeon Ghyll at the head of Great Langdale.*

OPPOSITE, RIGHT INSET: *A group of visiting country dancers perform outside the local hotel at Skelwith Bridge, near Ambleside.*

Kendal

Kendal is the main gateway to the Lakes for most travellers who come from the south. Now a prosperous town of 24000 people, its turbulent history is suggested by the many narrow courtyards which lead off the main street. These are reputed to have been constructed so that defence was easy in the time of border raids from Scotland. The ruined castle where Catherine Parr, sixth wife of Henry VIII, was born is a notable viewpoint, standing dominant on a green hill above the town. The grey limestone buildings of old Kendal cling together on the steep fellside to the west.

A fine parish church of the Holy Trinity dates back to the 13th century, and with its five aisles is one of the widest in the country. A musical carillon of tuneful bells can be heard marking the passing hours at the Town Hall. Pleasant riverside walks may be enjoyed at Gooseholme and in Abbot Hall park. Here there is also a good art gallery, and the award-winning Museum of Lakeland Life and Industry. The museum illustrates changes in rural and urban life in Lakeland over the past 200 years, giving a fascinating and helpful picture of the region as it used to be.

Today the thriving town industries range from shoe making to engineering, from snuff manufacture to mint cake production, and include pottery, printing and carpet weaving.

BELOW: *Tulip time in Maude's Meadow park, looking towards the church of St Thomas.*

Brockhole

Converted from a magnificent Victorian mansion overlooking the lake, the Lake District National Park Centre is located at Brockhole on the A591 road roughly halfway between Ambleside and Windermere. When it was opened in 1969 it was the first of its kind in England. The aim of the centre is to increase visitor awareness of the National Park.

A unique exhibition illustrates the natural and human changes which have contributed to the evolution of the Lake District into what it is today. From March to November a series of talks and films are given regularly, interspersed with special topics and celebrity lectures. Occasionally whole day meetings are devoted to one theme, with leading authorities taking part. There are extensive grounds of over 30 acres (12 ha) which sweep down to the lake shore. Formal gardens are especially noted for spring displays of rhododendrons and azaleas; open grassy picnic areas and a self-guided lakeshore walk are all included.

Longer excursions, led by Park Ranger staff who are experts on the region, may be enjoyed from Brockhole to nearby places of interest. Boat trips can be taken to Brockhole from Bowness and Waterhead, enjoying *en route* magnificent views across Windermere to the central Lakeland mountains. Any Brockhole visit becomes an attractive outing in glorious surroundings, and should contribute greatly to the enjoyment of a Lakeland holiday.

Windermere, Bowness and Ambleside

For many visitors the first sight of a lake is Windermere, a wide blue ribbon spread out below Claife Heights, viewed from the A591 road from Kendal. More than 10 miles (16 km) long, a mile (1.6 km) across, and over 200 feet (60 m) deep, it is by far the greatest natural expanse of fresh water in England. Users of the lake vary from large motor vessels – *Swan*, *Teal* and *Tern* – to small rowing boats and self-drive motor boats which may be hired at Bowness, Waterhead and Lakeside. A busy car ferry operates a regular service at the narrowest point of the lake near Bowness, giving attractive access to roads on the western shore leading to the villages of Sawrey and Hawkshead. Panoramas of Lakeland may be seen from the low hills of Orrest Head and Gummer's How.

At Bowness the ancient St Martin's church has notable stained glass, including the coat of arms of John Washington, later to be used in the American Stars and Stripes flag. The Roman fort of Galava is found near Ambleside, and the village also holds a rush-bearing ceremony each summer, together with a popular Lakeland sports meeting.

RIGHT: *The National Trust property of Bridge House, Ambleside, a unique 16th-century building on a bridge over Stock Ghyll.*

BELOW: *A Windermere 'steamer' leaves Lakeside on its 10-mile journey to Waterhead, passing Gummer's How at the start of the trip.*

OPPOSITE, LEFT INSET: *Typical Lakeland stone houses in Troutbeck village near Windermere.*

OPPOSITE, RIGHT INSET: *A golden sunrise across Waterhead Bay in Borrans Park, Ambleside.*

Lakeland Sports and Shows

At one time, each large village held its annual sports. This is not always the case now, but there are few Saturdays in July and August when sports meetings cannot be found somewhere in Cumbria. The traditional events, the spectacles unique to Lakeland, are those competitions which are only seen within the boundaries of the Lake District. The mighty trio are fell racing, hound trailing and wrestling in Cumberland and Westmorland style, the day's sport often combined with a local annual agricultural show.

The fell or 'guides' race is a race up the steepest nearby mountain from a flat arena in the valley bottom. A stern test of stamina and courage, the climb to the top of Butter Crags at Grasmere takes 10 minutes, and the descent two and a half. Another popular race is held at Ambleside, with smaller meetings at Loweswater, Buttermere,

Lowick and Rusland. Almost a vertical obstacle race, walls, gates, bracken and rocks have all to be skilfully negotiated by competitors at breakneck speed.

Hound trailing is another Lakeland speciality, and the sport is governed by the Hound Trailing Association, which authorises fixtures during the summer. Highly bred dogs are trained to follow scent across perhaps 10 miles of rugged mountain tracks. Two local men who know the ground have laid the trail, dragging a bundle of woollen rags soaked in paraffin, aniseed and turpentine. Trailers walk together to the mid-point and then separate, one laying the starting half and one the finishing section.

Lean baying dogs are held at the starting line by their owners, with 20 or more hounds setting off on their mountainous circuit. Betting is heavy, but guarded trails and marked dogs ensure that unscrupulous owners have small chance of success. Soon the runners will re-enter the arena, excited by a deafening chorus of whistles, shouts and halloos from the owners as their dogs race for the finishing tape.

Wrestling in Cumberland and Westmorland style goes on all day. This is a contest of strength, skill and agility. Traditional costume of white vest and tights, with embroidered velvet pants, is a 'must' at all top meetings; competitions for the best and

ABOVE: Hounds and owners at the start of a hound trail near Kendal.

LEFT: A trailer returns after laying a 'scent' for the hounds to follow over the hills.

OPPOSITE, ABOVE: A mountain-race winner clears a stone wall as he descends Loweswater Fell in the Vale of Lorton.

OPPOSITE, BELOW: Wrestling in Cumberland and Westmorland style at the Keswick Show in north Lakeland.

neatest outfits are often held prior to the actual wrestling.

Each pair is called by the bellman, steps out onto the grass, shakes hands and the bout begins, shoulder on shoulder, hands clasped behind the opponent's back. World championships are fought for on the green turf of the valleys, where a 16-stone (114 kg) farmer will begin his contest with the grace of a ballet dancer. A split second of violent action follows, and one man flies through the air, victim perhaps of a hank, a back heel or an inside hype. Loser is first to break the hold or to be thrown to the ground. A hundred or more spectacular contests may be fought in one day.

Village shows and fairs are an attractive summer feature in the Lakeland valleys. Often based on a local farming background, they can usually be visited in late summer and early autumn. Sheepdog trials often combine with the shows.

Grasmere and Rydal

Wordsworth and Grasmere are inseparable. From 1799 to 1808 Dove Cottage was the home of the premier poet of Lakeland. Here William Wordsworth wrote some of his greatest poetry and enjoyed by simple country living perhaps the happiest years of his adult life. Now owned by the trustees of Dove Cottage, this Lakeland house of stone, plaster and whitewashed walls has been carefully preserved largely as it was in Wordsworth's day.

The placid lake and surrounding hills were always a source of inspiration to the poet, and walks in the Grasmere area are especially rewarding. A circuit of the lake may be made, whilst an easy stroll to White Moss Common opens up viewpoints from which both Grasmere Lake and Rydal Water may be seen. The valley walk towards lonely Easedale Tarn is a popular route, particularly when the tumbling waterfalls of Sour Milk Ghyll are in spate.

On the Saturday nearest to St Oswald's Day (5 August) visitors to Grasmere are numbered in thousands. Their goal is the centuries old rush-bearing ceremony. This probably dates from the period when rushes were brought from the fields and lakeside to cover the church floor before winter. Today it is a purely decorative procession round the village, with brilliant flower garlands added to the green rushes. The church banner of St Oswald heads the ceremonial walk, with children in green costumes and white-robed clergymen adding further touches of colour to this traditional scene.

Two miles from Grasmere, the tiny village of Rydal is again associated with Wordsworth. Rydal Mount was his home from 1813 to 1850, and a field of daffodils, named in memory of Wordsworth's daughter Dora, can be found beside the road from Ambleside to Grasmere. The house itself contains family portraits, first editions and personal possessions of the poet, in a fine setting of landscaped gardens overlooking the lovely Vale of Rydal.

BELOW: Village children meet at St Oswald's church wall in Grasmere at the start of the rush-bearing ceremony.

OPPOSITE: A placid summer day on the lake at Grasmere, beneath the towering slopes of Nab Scar mountain in the background.

OPPOSITE, LEFT INSET: Rydal Mount, Wordsworth's home from 1813 to 1850.

OPPOSITE, RIGHT INSET: Dove Cottage, Grasmere, home of the poet William Wordsworth from 1799 to 1808.

Coniston, Hawkshead and Tarn Hows

This part of Lakeland has been home to many authors of national and international repute. Brantwood, on the eastern shore of Coniston Water, was the home of the celebrated Victorian poet, artist and writer John Ruskin. He lived here for 28 years, and the house is now preserved with much of his furniture, pictures and books still remaining.

At Hawkshead, William Wordsworth attended the grammar school and is reputed to have lodged at Ann Tyson's cottage nearby. Later the renowned children's author Beatrix Potter spent much of her life at Hill Top farm, Near Sawrey. The house is open to visitors and is one of the busiest National Trust properties in the region. Coniston Water is the venue for some of the popular Arthur Ransome sailing stories.

Later, Sir Malcolm Campbell and his son Donald used Coniston Water for speed-boat record attempts; a green stone memorial in the village perpetuates the memory of the latter after his death in a high-speed crash.

Near Hawkshead lies the beautiful National Trust property Tarn Hows. This upland tarn blends so well into its surroundings that it is hard to believe that it was created artificially by damming a stream. Edged with conifers and with circling footpaths, it gives fine panoramic views to the major Lakeland hills. Coniston Old Man, Wetherlam, the Langdale Pikes and Helvellyn are some renowned peaks which are viewed from here.

BELOW: *Coniston Water and the peak of Coniston Old Man, seen from the garden of Brantwood, home of the Victorian writer John Ruskin.*

OPPOSITE: *The National Trust's splendid steam yacht* Gondola *sails in summer on scheduled services across Coniston Water.*

INSET: *Hill Top at Near Sawrey, the home of the famous children's author Beatrix Potter.*

RIGHT: *Tarn Hows in autumn, looking towards the mountains of Helvellyn and Fairfield.*

Fell Walking and Rock Climbing

British mountaineering owes much to Lakeland, and the most popular valleys for climbers are Langdale, Wasdale, Borrowdale and Eskdale, lying at the foot of the major mountains.

Fell walking, with care, lies within the ability of most from 7 to 70 who are reasonably fit, but rock climbing calls for a special breed of men and women. Strength, balance, iron nerves and immaculate judgement are all needed if Dow Crag, Pavey Ark and Naples Needle are to be conquered. An apprenticeship should be served on easy beginners' climbs before the extremely severe ones are attempted, for such climbs stretch the best of each generation to the limit of their ability.

Most of the classic rock climbs lie west of a line from Ambleside to Keswick, using largely the crags of Borrowdale Volcanic rock. This surface is often rough, giving good hand and foot holds on massive precipices of sound rock. Semi-alpine conditions occur in winter, when work on snow and ice in north-facing gullies is a task for the expert climber.

Inevitably the challenge of the hills has brought competition, and for fell walkers the supreme test is the Bob Graham round. This involves climbing more than 40 Lakeland peaks over a distance of 75 miles (120 km), and with 27000 feet (8229 m) of ascent and descent. The record time for the circuit stands at 13 hours 54 minutes.

Going on the fells can never be without hazard, and one of the pioneers of climbing gave his opinion thus: 'Courage and strength are nought without prudence; do nothing in haste; look well to each step; and from the beginning, think what may be the end.' Mountain rescue on the hills is now highly organised, with voluntary search and rescue teams based at many points accessible to the hills. Highly mobile, with Landrovers and extensive rescue equipment, the teams co-operate with RAF helicopter services. Treat the mountains with respect, and they will give hours of immense enjoyment.

BELOW: A group of winter walkers follow the path over Huntingstile from Langdale to Grasmere.

ABOVE: *High summer on Harter Fell, overlooking Haweswater reservoir in eastern Lakeland.*

MOUNTAIN SAFETY

• **WEAR** brightly coloured, wind-and-rain-proof clothing. Strong leather boots with studded or non-slip soles are essential.

• **TAKE** map, compass, whistle, torch, spare food, warm clothing, watch, first-aid kit and at least one companion.

• **KNOW** how to use your map and compass, what time it gets dark and the distress signal for use in an emergency (6 long blasts or flashes repeated at one-minute intervals).

• **TELL** someone where you are going, and when and where you intend to return.

• **AVOID** precipices, icy slopes, loose boulders, gullies and stream beds, over-confidence and carelessness.

RIGHT: *Rock climbing on Raven Crag, Great Langdale.*

Places to Visit

CENTRAL LAKELAND

Houses
Brantwood, by Coniston Water. Home of John Ruskin.

Dove Cottage, Grasmere. Home of William Wordsworth.

Hill Top, Near Sawrey. Home of Beatrix Potter.

Rydal Mount, near Ambleside. Wordsworth's last home.

Townend, Troutbeck. 17th-century farmhouse with original furnishings.

Gardens
Holehird, near Windermere.

Stagshaw, near Ambleside.

Museums and Visitor Centres
Brockhole, National Park Visitor Centre, near Windermere.

Grizedale Forest Visitor Centre, near Hawkshead.

Windermere Steamboat Museum, Windermere.

Wordsworth Museum, Town End, Grasmere.

NORTH LAKELAND

Castle and Cathedral
Carlisle Castle. 12th-century keep, 13th-century gatehouse.

Carlisle Cathedral. Norman and Early English, with magnificent 14th-century east end.

Gardens
Corby Castle, Wetheral, near Carlisle.

Lingholm, by Derwentwater.

Museums and Visitor Centre
Border Regiment Museum, Carlisle.

Carlisle Museum. Cumbrian natural history, archaeology (especially the Roman wall) and fine arts.

Fitz Park Museum, Keswick. Manuscripts of Southey, Wordsworth, Coleridge and Walpole, and local geology and natural history.

Thornthwaite Visitor Centre, Whinlatter Pass, near Keswick. Forest trails and displays of forestry landscapes and life.

SOUTH LAKELAND

Castles, Houses and Priory
Cartmel Priory. Church of 12th-century foundation, with fine 15th-century carving; impressive 14th-century gatehouse.

Holker Hall, Cark-in-Cartmel. See page 32.

Kendal Castle. Ruined birthplace of Catherine Parr, dating from 12th century onwards.

Levens Hall, near Kendal. See page 32.

Rusland Hall, near Ulverston. Georgian, features mechanical music in 18th-century surroundings.

Sizergh Castle, near Kendal. 14th-century pele tower, with 15th-century great hall, and later additions. See page 32.

Swarthmoor Hall, Ulverston. Elizabethan home of George Fox, who founded the Society of Friends.

Gardens
Graythwaite Hall, near Newby Bridge.

Holker Hall, Cark-in-Cartmel.

Levens Hall, near Kendal.

Art Gallery and Museums
Abbot Hall Art Gallery, Kendal. Georgian building featuring 18th-century furniture and paintings, including Romney's *The Gower Family*.

Kendal Museum. Outstanding mammal and bird collection, local geology and relics of early man.

Museum of Lakeland Life and Industry, Kendal.

EAST LAKELAND

Castles and Houses
Appleby Castle. Norman keep and medieval buildings; conservation centre for rare British farm animals.

Brough Castle, near Kirkby Stephen. Norman keep on a Roman site, with later additions.

Brougham Castle, near Penrith. Ruined 12th-century keep and other buildings on the site of a Roman fort.

Dalemain, near Penrith. Medieval, Elizabethan and Georgian houses; agricultural and yeomanry museums. See page 32.

Hutton-in-the-Forest, near Penrith. 14th-century pele tower, with later additions; pictures, tapestries, furniture and gardens.

Garden
Acorn Bank, Temple Sowerby, near Penrith.

WEST LAKELAND

Castles and House
Cockermouth Castle. 13th and 14th-century ruins.

Egremont Castle. Early Norman site. 12th-century ruins.

Muncaster Castle, near Ravenglass. See page 32.

Wordsworth House, Cockermouth. Poet's birthplace.

Museums
Whitehaven Museum. Archaeology, industrial history, geology, mining and nautical items.

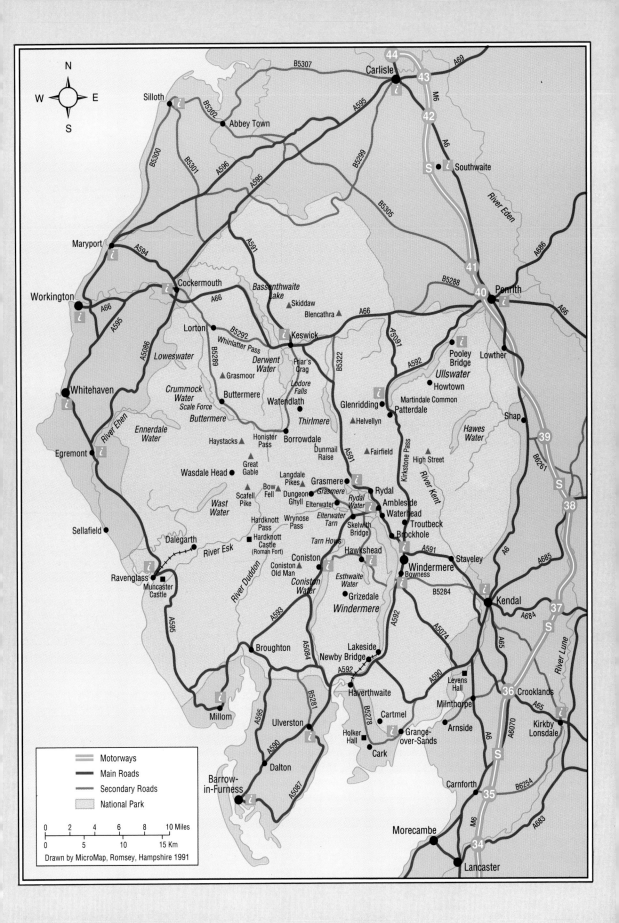

Langdale, Loughrigg and Elterwater

The Langdale valley is generally recognised as one of the finest in Lakeland, and with easy access from the south through Ambleside it is one of the most popular holiday areas. Beyond Skelwith Bridge, with its well-known waterfall, the road winds through leafy woodlands above the shores of Elterwater Tarn.

A diversion from Skelwith Bridge along the lower slopes of Loughrigg Fell leads to Loughrigg Tarn, a tiny mirror-like sheet of water almost encircled by trees, and with an easy footpath along the shore. Walkers may

continue along Loughrigg Terrace to Grasmere or Rydal, whilst the motorist may descend Red Bank into Grasmere or return to the Langdale valley at Elterwater. The village green here encircles a picturesque maple tree.

From all directions, the twin peaks of the Langdale Pikes dominate the scene. Not high, even by Lakeland standards, at 2403 feet (732m), the slopes rise abruptly from the valley floor at Dungeon Ghyll. Their craggy outlines form a typical view even when seen from 10 miles (16km) distant.

ABOVE: *Elterwater Tarn and Langdale Pikes.*

OPPOSITE, ABOVE LEFT: *Langdale Valley, Bowfell and Lingmoor.*

OPPOSITE, ABOVE RIGHT: *Skelwith Waterfall, between Ambleside and Langdale.*

OPPOSITE, CENTRE RIGHT: *Loughrigg Tarn, on the lower slopes of Loughrigg Fell.*

The village houses at Elterwater and Chapel Stile are built from grey-green stone quarried in the valley, where the slate industry has been the main occupation for centuries. Stone in Langdale was worked 5000 years ago at a Stone Age axe factory situated near Pike of Stickle, and axes have been found at various sites throughout England. It is hard to imagine that the peaceful village of Elterwater was once a noted centre for gunpowder making, using water power from the river and local charcoal from the surrounding coppice woods.

From Chapel Stile the road winds westward to Dungeon Ghyll. This is another famous rock-climbing centre, with Gimmer Crag and Pavey Ark near at hand. For the fell walker there is the circuit of the Langdale horseshoe around Bowfell and Harrison Stickle. A steep mountain pass over Blea Tarn links the valleys of Great and Little Langdale, where the blue waters of Blea Tarn gleam invitingly against the dark crags of Blake Rigg. Blea Tarn house nearby is the residence of 'The Solitary' in Wordsworth's poem *The Excursion*.

LEFT: *Blea Tarn and Harrison Stickle.*

Steam in Lakeland

Perhaps in reaction against the pace of modern living, there seems to be increasing nostalgia for the more leisurely steam travel of former years. In Lakeland both railway and boat enthusiasts are well catered for.

A visit to the Ravenglass and Eskdale miniature railway is a fascinating glimpse of the age of steam. This 15-inch (381mm) gauge line, almost 7 miles (11km) in length, is the successor to trains of 3-foot (914mm) gauge which ran over 100 years ago. Today the route from Ravenglass to Dalegarth is served by four steam engines, picturesquely named after three rivers which meet at Ravenglass. The *River Esk, River Irt* and *River Mite*, together with the *Northern Rock*, provide a unique trip on a narrow-gauge steam line from the sea to the foothills of great mountains. A combined ramble and ride excursion is popular with

walkers in the valley, using intermediate stations at the start or finish of the outing.

For the boat enthusiast, the place to go is the Windermere Steamboat Museum. Opened by Prince Charles in 1977, this is a collection of early steam craft. Pride of place probably goes to the steam launch *Dolly*, built around 1850 and generally recognised as the oldest mechanically propelled boat in the world. Second to her is the steam yacht *Esperance*, the oldest boat on Lloyd's Yacht Register; for elegance, the 80-year-old steam launch *Branksome* must lead, with woodwork in teak and walnut and with its original velvet and leather upholstery. Up to 30 boats can be berthed in the steamboat dock, and a large display area provides additional information. Lake cruises under steam are available on the steam-powered launches *Osprey, Swallow* and *Kittiwake*. On Coniston

ABOVE: *Gaily decorated vessels of the Windermere Steamboat Museum moored on their lakeside jetties.*

OPPOSITE, ABOVE LEFT: *An exhibit at the annual Cumbria Steam Gathering is lovingly polished.*

OPPOSITE, ABOVE RIGHT: *A standard-gauge steam train leaves Haverthwaite station on its journey to Lakeside.*

OPPOSITE, BELOW: *Full steam ahead at Muncaster Mill station on the Ravenglass and Eskdale railway.*

Water the National Trust large steam yacht *Gondola* sails, restored to all its Victorian splendour years after being abandoned as a sunken wreck. Regular cruises in summer link the piers at Coniston, Park-a-Moor and Brantwood.

For standard-gauge steam trains one must visit the south end of Windermere at Lakeside. This is the terminus of the three and a half mile (5km) long Haverthwaite to Newby Bridge railway. From this branch line of the former Furness railway, trains connect at Lakeside with passenger boats on Windermere, giving an attractive route into Lakeland.

No steam enthusiast visiting Lakeland should omit a visit to Steamtown at Carnforth. This is the largest mainline steam locomotive depot in Britain. Normally more than 20 British and Continental mainline and industrial locomotives are on view, with some 'in steam' at weekends from March to October. The mile (1.6km) long site includes some of the working equipment of the former Carnforth Motive Power Depot, one of the latest railway areas in the country to retain steam locomotives. The Cumbria Steam Gathering at Cark, near Flookburgh, often attracts 500 exhibits.

ABOVE: *Birks Bridge on the River Duddon.*

BELOW: *The Roman fort of Mediobogdum, or Hardknott Castle, located near the Hardknott Pass road from the Duddon Valley to Eskdale.*

Eskdale and the Duddon Valley

Two of the finest beauty spots of western Lakeland are provided by the Duddon and Eskdale valleys. Unusually for Lakeland, they are both lakeless, but make up for this by their streams, which are like mountain torrents. Crystal clear, with every stone visible on the stream bed, they provide along their banks some of the most attractive picnic spots that one could find when yellow gorse spills over the river worn boulders in June, or brown bracken enriches the valleys on a fine October day.

Between the two valleys one can travel the renowned Hardknott Pass, with hairpin bends and one-in-three gradients, a test for both car and driver. Alongside the road on the Eskdale side is the ruined fort of Mediobogdum, home of a Roman garrison almost 2000 years ago.

At the mouth of the Esk is the attractive small harbour of Ravenglass, with colour washed cottages huddled together near the shore. The dunes at Ravenglass were desig-

nated a nature reserve in 1954, and now support the largest colony of black-headed gulls in England together with Sandwich and Arctic terns, shelducks and oyster-catchers as residents or visitors.

Wasdale and Ennerdale

Wasdale's remote western valley has many claims to fame. England's highest mountain peak, Scafell Pike, at 3210 feet (978m), is adjacent to the shores of the deepest lake, Wastwater, 258 feet (78m) deep. On the south-east side the famous screes sweep down from Illgill Head into the depths of the lake, whilst the opposite western shore is a place for outings and picnics as the July sun warms rocks and shingle.

Always one's view is drawn towards the circling peaks at the valley head, Yewbarrow, Kirk Fell, Great Gable and Scafell, the epitome of Lakeland landscape; this view of Wastwater and Gable was chosen as the emblem of the Lake District National Park.

The hamlet of Wasdale Head is a Mecca for fell walkers and mountaineers. High-level passes lead to the Ennerdale, Buttermere, Borrowdale, Langdale and Eskdale valleys, with top-grade rock climbs on Pillar, Gable and Scafell all within easy reach. A fine horseshoe circuit for experienced walkers is the route around Mosedale, starting near the narrow packhorse bridge. One of Lakeland's smallest churches is found at Wasdale Head, flanked by its sheltering yew trees in a setting of supreme mountain grandeur. Many of the memorials in its tiny churchyard bear witness to the fatal fascination which the surrounding peaks have long exercised over climbers.

The remote valley of Ennerdale is perhaps one of the most peaceful spots in the Lake District. Traffic restrictions apply beyond a car park near Ennerdale Water, and there is no through road after this point. Climbers' venues of Steeple and Pillar Rock attract the mountaineer, with a long approach path via quiet forestry tracks, passing waymarked nature trails *en route.*

RIGHT: *Ennerdale Water looking towards Steeple and Pillar Rock.*

Buttermere and Crummock Water

Twin lakes sharing the same valley, Buttermere and Crummock Water, will appeal especially to the lover of peace and quiet. No power-boats disturb their surface, although rowing boats, canoes and small sailing craft are permitted. The approach from Honister Pass and Borrowdale on a road reaching 1176 feet (358m) above sea level passes one of Lakeland's highest youth hostels, whilst on the left the face of Honister Crag has been honeycombed with caves and tunnels through years of quarrying for its valuable slate.

The Honister summit is now widely used as a starting point for many fell walks; the route from here to Great Gable is popular, and there is an easy climb with many rewarding views to the tarn-studded summit of nearby Haystacks.

Fleetwith Pike towers above the pass as it nears Buttermere. High Crag, High Stile and Red Pike all lie to the west, whilst Robinson,Whiteless Pike and Grasmoor match them in grandeur on the east. Scale Force is a well-known destination for excursions from Buttermere village, and its waterfall of cascading torrents is the highest in Lakeland (172 feet, 52m). North of Crummock the gentler landscape of the Vale of Lorton is soon visible, and the blue gem of tiny Loweswater lies beside a minor road leading westwards.

ABOVE: *Autumn sunlight on the beeches at Buttermere.*

OPPOSITE: *Morning reflections at Crummock Water.*

OPPOSITE, LEFT INSET: *Loweswater seen from the summit of Mellbreak.*

OPPOSITE, RIGHT INSET: *Gorse in springtime on the shores of Crummock Water, looking towards Red Pike.*

Keswick, Derwentwater and Watendlath

Keswick is by far the most popular centre from which to visit the northern part of Lakeland. Few spots in England can be more attractively placed, for it lies at the foot of Skiddaw and extends almost to the shore of Derwentwater. A prominent landmark in the town centre is the Moot Hall, built over 100 years ago on the site of an earlier (16th-century) foundation.

The 18th and 19th centuries saw the first notable authors 'discovering' Lakeland, with Coleridge living at Keswick in 1800, followed three years later by the poet Robert Southey. Other famous visitors at this time included Shelley, Scott, Hazlitt and Lamb, seeking perhaps the peace so well portrayed by Thomas Gray, writing in 1769: 'In the evening I walked alone down to the lake …after sunset, and saw the solemn colouring of the night draw on, the last gleam of sunshine fading away on the hilltops, the deep serene of the waters, and the long shadows of the mountains' (*Tour of the Lakes*).

The National Trust owns the famous beauty spot of Friar's Crag, where memorials to John Ruskin, the writer, and Canon Rawnsley, one of the Trust's founders, are located on the craggy headland amongst the pine trees. Swimming, fishing and boating may all be fully enjoyed at Derwentwater, or walks to easily accessible viewpoints nearby, such as Castle Head, with its fine prospect of the lake, or to the Lodore Falls.

A well-known outing from Keswick is to the hamlet of Watendlath, used by Sir Hugh Walpole as the background setting for his ever popular *Herries Chronicles* series of novels. On the way the famous Ashness Bridge is reached, beloved of artists and photographers. Shortly afterwards, a detour on the right leads to a wooded precipice, commonly known as 'Surprise View'. The crag falls almost to the shore of Derwentwater, with cars and motor launches appearing as toys, hundreds of feet below. Watendlath itself shelters in a deep hollow amongst the hills, hidden in its 'secret' valley beside the blue Watendlath Tarn. From here an easy footpath leads over the hills to Rosthwaite in Borrowdale. It gives fine views towards the highest peaks of the Lake District.

Farming in Lakeland

Today's landscape in the valley heads of Lakeland owes its appearance to volcanoes, glaciers and the Cumbrian sheep farmer. The volcanoes provided the tough Borrowdale Volcanic rock from which most of the central fells are made, and the glaciers carved the valleys, radiating from a central dome like the spokes of a wheel. The sheep farmer has tamed what was left.

One of the first tasks was to enclose and fence the wilderness, and some of this was done when the monasteries were the great local landowners. The walls are built from the native rock, gathered from nearby fields and fellsides. Most of the walls, clinging to the hills like long grey caterpillars, are dry-stone walls. No mortar is used, only the rock to form two wall faces with a rubble core in between. Here and there a gigantic 'through' stone is placed, going from one side to the other, with a line of stone cams along the top. Built largely during the enclosure period of the early 19th century, the walls climb to fell summits 1000 feet (305m) or more high, mute testimony to the skills of men who laboured long ago.

With land as rough, soil as thin and climate as wet as those of central Lakeland, sheep and hill cattle have to provide the main source of farming income. The sheep which thrives so well here is the grey-faced Herdwick, unique to the central sheep farms. Its origin is lost in the mists of the past, but its introduction to Lakeland has been attributed to Norse farmers who settled here, or to its having been washed ashore from shipwrecks of the Spanish Armada. Tough, sure-footed and hardy, the Herdwick will graze on the highest summits, each flock keeping close to its own 'heaf', or regular grazing area. Flock marking is essential to sort out the strays, and each farm has its own personal earmark and smitmark recorded in the *Shepherd's Guide*.

BELOW: *Sheep-gathering on the Howgill Fells of east Cumbria, where the last snows of winter linger on the summits.*

Shearing takes place about July, often a task shared between neighbours, and clipping time is one of the busiest seasons on a farm. A fleece may weigh around 5 pounds (2kg) and this strong, coarse, grey wool often ends up as a carpet, or hard-wearing tweed. Flocks of 500 Herdwick ewes are not uncommon, together with Swaledale and Rough Fell breeds on the farms away from the central mountains. In summer, open days are held on various farms throughout Lakeland, when visitors are shown over the land and farming methods explained. Autumn brings many different village shows, when the 'Blue Riband' for a hill farmer is to win with his sheep at Eskdale, Wasdale or Lowick.

Traditional sheepdog trials are often held in the quieter months of late summer. There are three principal meetings, at Ings near Windermere, Rydal and Patterdale. The competition is to gather, drive and pen about five reluctant and unco-operative animals. Success demands the utmost in skill and rapport between dog and shepherd. Stick making competitions are often held at each meeting, when craftsmen exhibit ornamental shepherds' crooks. The handles are decorated with the intricate horn carvings of birds and animals, attached to a burnished stem of holly or hazel wood.

ABOVE, LEFT: *A typical Lakeland white-washed farmhouse at Yewdale, near Coniston.*

ABOVE, RIGHT: *Old-fashioned hand shearing may still be found in some of the more remote valleys.*

LEFT: *Dry-stone walling to repair a gap at Patterdale.*

Ullswater, Thirlmere and Haweswater

Second to Windermere in size, Ullswater is one of the leading lakes for the boating and yachting enthusiast. It extends in three reaches from Pooley Bridge in the north to Glenridding and Patterdale in the south, a distance of over 7 miles (11km). The Patterdale end has fine mountain scenery, being surrounded by Helvellyn, Fairfield and Place Fell. The waterfall of Aira Force is popular with visitors, and from nearby Gowbarrow Park the well wooded shores and steep mountain sides provide ever changing views, to be seen to perfection in June greenery or amidst the rich browns of golden autumn.

The quiet lake held great attractions for Wordsworth, and his famous poem *The Daffodils* is generally recognised as having been written about the wild daffodils along Ullswater's shore.

Thirlmere and Haweswater, although 10 miles (16km) apart and separated by two ranges of mountains, are both lakes which became the first great reservoirs of Manchester. The former lies along the busy Ambleside to Keswick road, but a discerning visitor will choose the peace of a scenic route along the western shore.

Remote on the eastern fringe of Lakeland, the Haweswater valley still retains some of its former isolation, guarded by the crags around High Street, unchanged since traversed by Roman soldiers almost 2000 years ago.

ABOVE: *Late afternoon sunlight gleams through fine beech trees on Ullswater's shore near Glenridding.*

OPPOSITE: *Haweswater in eastern Lakeland, seen from the summit of Harter Fell, at the head of the Longsleddale valley.*

LEFT: *The southern reach of Ullswater, from a viewpoint at Yew Crag in the National Trust property of Gowbarrow Park.*

RIGHT: *Thirlmere and the peak of Helvellyn, from the scenic road on the west side of the lake.*

Stately Homes in Lakeland

Many stately homes with attractive gardens exist in and around Lakeland; they range from small farmhouses of the Middle Ages to huge castles built and restored over many centuries.

Holker Hall, near Grange-over-Sands, has extensive gardens with many rare shrubs and trees, whilst the house contains fine paintings, furniture and carvings. At Levens Hall, south of Kendal, garden features include topiary work on ancient yew trees, and paths laid out in the original 17th-century pattern. In west Cumbria near Ravenglass, Muncaster Castle's gardens include one of Europe's finest collections of rhododendrons and azaleas. Sizergh Castle near Kendal is a National Trust property which features a 14th-century pele tower and 15th-century great hall. Dalemain near Penrith is noted for its combination of medieval, Elizabethan and Georgian architecture blended together in one building, in an attractive parkland setting.

ABOVE: *Holker Hall and gardens, near Grange-over-Sands in south Cumbria.*

LEFT: *Sizergh Castle in autumn, viewed across the ornamental lake.*